LIFE'S A GATECRASH

by

TERRY HUGHES

Published by Playdead Press 2014

© Terry Hughes 2014

Terry Hughes have asserted their rights under the Copyright, Design and Patents Act, 1988, to be identified as the author of this work.

A CIP catalogue record for this book is available from the British Library.

ISBN 978-1-910067-17-8

Caution
All rights whatsoever in this play are strictly reserved and application for performance should be sought through the author before rehearsals begin. No performance may be given unless a license has been obtained.

This book is sold subject to the condition that it shall not by way of trade or otherwise, be lent, resold, hired out, or otherwise circulated without the publisher's prior consent in any form of binding or cover other than that in which it is published and without a similar condition including this condition being imposed on the subsequent purchaser.

Printed by BPUK

Playdead Press
www.playdeadpress.com

Life's a Gatecrash was first produced at the Edinburgh Festival, at C venue 19 on 6th August 1997 with the following cast:

Steve	Ian Holmes
Nicola	Helen Copley
Phil	James Foster
Sid	Richard Boyce
Director	Julio Maria Martino

This production of *Life's a Gatecrash* was shown by PACT Productions at the King's Arms Studio, Salford on the 22nd July 2014 with the following cast:

Steve	Eddie Capli
Nicola	Joise Walsh
Phil	Paddy Byrne
Sid	Lewis Marsh
Director	Andy Pope

CAST

Eddie Capli | Steve

Eddie is the co-founder of PACT productions and has a strong passion to bring original and topical writing to the forefront of fringe theatre. Although Eddie has appeared in all of PACTs productions he maintains consistent roles outside of the company within role play and radio work and has recently performed opposite Tom Courtenay in the Radio Academy Award winning *Lost and Found*. Last year Eddie appeared in *Night on the Field of Waterloo* for The Manchester 24/7 Theatre festival and since then has been excited by the prospect of bringing some of the work PACT has to offer to the festival scene. Aside from all the new plays Eddie has been involved with, he has also just written, produced and acted in a new short film entitled *Fridays Detention*. Theatre includes: *The Call* (Pact Productions); *Night On The Field Of Waterloo* (Near Run Thing Theatre); *Evening Star* (Pact Productions); Radio includes: *Lost and Found*; *Tittle Tattle*; *Sochi (Living The Dream)*; *Art, Artefacts and Angels* (BBC Radio 4)

Josie Walsh | Nicola

Josie is currently a student at Act Up North - having attended various drama workshop. Theatre includes; *A Civilised Man; The Seagull* (The Lowry Theatre); *A Mid-Summer Nights Dream* (Open air Plas Coch) *My Method Man; Inspired* (Three Minute Theatre) *Gunfight at the Bullet Creek Saloon*, (Saint Anthonys Theatre); *The House of Bernada Alba* (Greenhill Dramatic Society)

Paddy Bryne | Phil

Hailing from Liverpool Paddy's acting career started at the age of 28 when he attained a BA in Theatre Studies and a Master of Arts in Screenwriting. Theatre includes: *A Midsummer Night's Dream* (The Actors Lab). Film includes: *Addict* (Street Wise Productions); *Donner Kebab* (Kicking Heal Productions); *Woof Ticket* (Mackykid Productions); *Top of the Range* (Belly Productions); *The Temp* (TV Plus Films); *The Six Sided Man* (Packer Productions); *The Thing About Being a Man* (Mend Productions); *Domino* (First Take Productions) Take Stock (Toxeth TV); *Dancing Queen* (First take Productions); *Hearing Voices* (Mac Productions); *Identity* (Elementary Productions); Toilet (Liverpool University); *Emily* (First Take Productions); *Porc Peis Bac* (Cambrensis Communications).

Lewis Marsh | Sid

Theatre includes: *A Night on the Field of Waterloo* (Manchester 24/7 Theatre Festival); *Light Through Every Window* (Lowry Studio Theatre and North West Tour); *Street Child* (Cotton Grass Theatre and National Tour); *Twelfth Night* (Cotton Grass Theatre, Thornbridge Hall); *Rid the World* (Lowry Studio Theatre and North West Tour); *Nice* (Ensemble 52, for 'Not Part Festival'); *The Merchant of Venice* (Demi Paradise Production, Lancaster Castle); *Human Habitation* (Studio Salford); *Out of Dead Air* (Manchester 24/7 Theatre Festival); *Now Breath Out* (Studio Salford); *Nico Icon Play* (The Lowry); *Richard III* (Studio Salford); *Concrete Ribbons* (The Library Theatre); *Six Characters in Search of an Author* (The Lowry); *Harlequin*; *Owen Parker* (Manchester 24/7 Theatre Festival); *Homelands* (Bolton Octagon); *Antigone* (Scene Productions-Tour); *Henry IV Part 1* (Edinburgh Festival). Television includes: *Heartbeat* (ITV); *Children's Ward* (Granada Television). Film includes: *Poor Wee Me; The World According to Liam Lovelle* (Looking Glass Film) *Kiddo* (SixSevenFour Productions)

Andy Pope | Director

Andy is the co-founder of PACT productions. Andy is a trained and working actor. He has been honing his writing skills and has written mainly comedic pieces with Davenport Productions since 2008. While writing, directing and performing theatre workshops for young people Andy and Eddie decided to create PACT. Opening with his debut play, *Evening Star* he hopes to continue to develop as a writer and actor, drawing influence from his home for the past 20 years, the creative and vibrant City that is Manchester. "Some 15 years ago I played the role of Sid in Terry Hughes' play *Life's a Gatecrash*. The impact of the piece, it's visceral language and knife edge tension has remained with me over the years. When PACT were searching for their next production I had no hesitation in suggesting 'Gatecrash' and am delighted to be directing this revival at the Kings Arms Theatre, Salford."

Terry Hughes | Writer

Terry Hughes is a playwright and director living and working in Manchester. Up until recently he was writer on attachment at the Octagon Theatre, Bolton where he most recently co-adapted J M Barrie's *Peter Pan* and Frank Baum's *The Wonderful Wizard of OZ* for the main theatre; most recent productions include *Crabs* (Soho Theatre); *Thing called Love* (Octagon Theatre, Bolton); *The Piece* (Lowry Theatre).

PACT PRODUCTIONS
~ Theatre at the heart of Manchester ~
Contact PACT- enquiries@pactproductions.com
www.pactproductions.com

ACT ONE

NIGHT. FLAT. STEVE and NICOLA burst in.

STEVE	What the fuck. What am I gonna... stupid fuckin arsehole. He just walked right out in front of me the stupid twat. Shit. I'm fucked man. Did you see that woman in the middle of the road, where'd she come from? I'm in shit if they... if that woman took my number... I saw her in the mirror, she was definitely, definitely looking to take my registration number.

NICOLA	You shoulda stopped you fuckin arsehole.

STEVE	What? Course. I know that? I know that now, don't I? I didn't though did I, no I fuckin carried on. Oh shit, mother of fuckin mercy man, I am fucked.

NICOLA	What's the matter with you? What came over you? Why did you keep on going? Jesus Christ Steve.

STEVE	I dunno do I. Some... something uncontrollable. I panicked didn't I, I couldn't help it.

NICOLA   It's not hard, not difficult. You run someone over and you stop the car, you apply the bloody breaks, you don't just carry on as if nothing's happened.

STEVE   It's no good telling me that now, is it? I mean, it's too late for that now, don't tell me that now you silly bitch.

NICOLA   Don't take it out on me.

STEVE thinks for a moment

STEVE   I could go back. Back to the scene. Where it happened.

NICOLA   Bit late for that, the police will be there an everything. You shoulda stopped when you had the chance.

STEVE   But I didn't did I. Why didn't I? What's going on? I dunno what came over me. What an arsehole. I couldn't help it though could I? I mean, you saw him, he just walked out in front of me, I didn't have a chance, what chance did I have?

NICOLA   You weren't concentrating.

STEVE   You what?

NICOLA   You weren't looking where you were going. As usual.

STEVE   Fuck you.

NICOLA   You can't blame him, he was just trying to cross the road.

STEVE   He didn't give me a chance.

NICOLA   You had plenty of time.

STEVE   You what?

NICOLA   You're not going to tell me that.

STEVE   What?

NICOLA   Just don't alright... jus... just don't.

STEVE   Don't what? What you on about?

NICOLA   You.

STEVE   What about me?

NICOLA stops herself

NICOLA   Forget it.

STEVE   No, what about me, come on?

NICOLA   Look, just back off will ya.

STEVE   You saw him. He didn't give me a chance.

NICOLA   Right.

NICOLA is silent

STEVE   Or maybe you think it's my fault.

NICOLA   Look, I'm not gonna lie to ya and tell ya you're the innocent party here. You were well over the limit and on top of that you weren't concentrating.

STEVE   Weren't concentrating?

NICOLA   No.

STEVE   An why was that?

NICOLA   Because you were shouting at me.

STEVE   Right.

NICOLA   So now it's my fault?

STEVE   If you hadn't distracted me... I mean if you... I dunno... you get on my tit's you know... I mean sometimes you get me like, really fucked up, really pissed off. You're there beside me bending me earhole about something or other all the time. How could anyone concentrate with that going on? You was having a go since we left the party. You're a fuckin cunt, that's the short of it.

NICOLA   You arsehole.

STEVE   Fuck you. Just fuck you.

Pause

STEVE   What am I gonna do? Shall I... do you think I should... do you reckon it's too late to... sort it... get it sorted?

Pause

STEVE   Maybe I killed... eh, maybe I killed that bloke. Nicky.

NICOLA   What.

STEVE   That bloke. Maybe he's dead. I might've killed him. I hit him hard. Full on. And I was going some as well. Jesus Christ, he went right over the fuckin top of me. I didn't even see him land, it all happened so quick.

Pause

STEVE   I should get it sorted. I might've killed that bloke. I better get it sorted out tonight. I should phone the old bill, right now, tell em the whole story. Shouldn't I? Nicky!

NICOLA   What?

STEVE   I should own up. Go down the police station, tell em what happened. I mean... he might be alright... maybe he's alright... maybe he's... Why didn't I stop the car? What's going on? What the fuck... made me not stop? Shit. If I... if I've... Oh well, whatever happens if I'm done I'm fucked. If I own up and I'm done, that's it, I'm fucked, they'll throw the fuckin book at me and no mistake. I'll go down. Oh, Christ Almighty I've killed someone, it's murder, I'll go down, fuck I'll go down. Why wasn't I... why didn't I... It was an accident. What the fuck was he doing in the middle of the road like that? He might've been pissed up. Eh, if he was pissed up it wasn't my fault, I mean I-

NICOLA   But you were well over the limit too, Steve.

STEVE   What?

NICOLA   He wasn't driving a car.

STEVE   So.

NICOLA   Look, you were in a state, you were all over the place. You were drunk when we left the party.

STEVE   No, I weren't.

NICOLA   You shouldn't have even been driving state you was in.

STEVE   I can drive. I'm a better driver when I've had a drink. It wasn't anything to do with me having a couple of shandies.

NICOLA   Sure.

STEVE   Look. You're supposed to be on my side.

NICOLA   What?

STEVE   You... You're-

NICOLA   Don't drag me into this.

STEVE   Why not? You was in the car as well.

NICOLA   So?

STEVE   Well that makes you liable or something. An accomplice.

NICOLA   I wasn't driving.

STEVE   No, but it was your fault.

NICOLA   My fault?

STEVE   Yea.

NICOLA   What you talking about?

STEVE   Don't play the innocent.

NICOLA   You're outa your fuckin mind. Fuck you.

NICOLA moves away but STEVE grabs her

STEVE   No, no, wait.

NICOLA   Let me go… let go of me you bastard.

STEVE   Just wait a minute… just hold on.

NICOLA   Let me go.

STEVE   Don't run away.

NICOLA   Let. Me. Go.

STEVE   Where you going? Where you gonna go?

NICOLA   Let me go you arsehole.

STEVE   It was you're fault.

NICOLA   You're hurting me.

STEVE   It was your fault.

NICOLA   Let me go I said.

STEVE   Wasn't it?

STEVE   Yea, it was my fault.

STEVE   Who's fault?

NICOLA   My fault.

STEVE   I know it was.

STEVE lets her go

STEVE   Shouldn't shout at me like that. You're always shouting at me. That's why I hit that bloke, I'd nowhere else to go, you got me like me head was coming off, right in me ear.

Pause

NICOLA   I know what you did.

STEVE   Do you?

NICOLA   You're an arsehole.

STEVE   Oh, yea.

NICOLA   Don't... just don't insult my intelligence, alright.

STEVE   What you on about?

Pause

NICOLA   It wasn't an accident, was it?

STEVE   Hum? Pardon?

NICOLA   Look. I know what you did. I know what happened, it happened in front of me, alright.

STEVE   What're you talking about?

NICOLA   That bloke. You did it on purpose. It wasn't an accident was it? Alright, so I was having a go at you but you could've avoided that man easily, you had plenty of time.

STEVE   No.

NICOLA   You actually swerved to hit him.

STEVE   No.

NICOLA   I saw it. I saw it all. You wanted to hit him. You actually went out of your way to hit him.

STEVE   It was an accident.

NICOLA   Come on admit it you-

STEVE   I'd had a few. I didn't know what I was doing. I was arseholed.

NICOLA   You were pissed off with me.

STEVE   Yea.

NICOLA   You were pissed off with me and you took it out on that man.

Pause

STEVE   Do you think I did it on purpose, is that what you're saying? Fuckin hell, come on, what. That I'd jus... that I'd just... run someone over like that... I... suddenly there he was, what could I do, fuckin dickhead.

Pause

STEVE   He was asking for it, walking out in the middle of the road like that. He was on a death wish... dangerous... causes accidents... innocent people killed or maimed... better off without his sort... drunk old bastard... getting in my way... we could've been killed... us... what the fuck... he deserved what he got... I hope I... Yea, yea, yea, yea I did.

Pause

             Everything just exploded. For a split second I really wanted him dead, really wanted to hurt something... someone. But that old bloke... who cares... I mean... who's gonna miss him when he's gone... fuck him off. I'm sorry. I should go to the police.

NICOLA   What now?

STEVE   No time like the present. I'm sure that bitch took me number as I drove off. I saw her in the mirror. There was so much going on so quickly, it all happened so fast. Best try and clear it up before they trace the motor. Maybe if I go down an admit it all now, face the music, it might look better in court, maybe I'll get a lighter sentence. What do you think?

Pause

NICOLA   I can't believe it. I can't believe you did that.

STEVE   I know I...

NICOLA   You're... I...

Pause

STEVE fills the kettle and switches it on. He drops tea-bags into cups, pours milk etc. They both wait in silence for the kettle to boil. The sound of the kettle coming to boil grows louder and louder. When it has boiled STEVE casually makes tea. Gives a cup to NICOLA

STEVE How fast do you think I was going? Not fast was it? Couldn't have been more than thirty. I slowed down just before... when he first walked out... it was only after that I put me foot down. Did you see him land? I hit him hard. He hit the windscreen... then I reversed and... he fell onto the road... then I... then I...

NICOLA Then you drove over him again.

STEVE That's right. That's right, I drove over him again. Oh Christ. I think I must've dragged him under... I definitely felt something underneath. Shit... that woman. She was quite old by the look of her... and... and it was dark... I mean... there weren't any streetlights were there? And I mean I... And I sped off quick... well... very quick in fact, she may not have seen much at all. I mean... it would've been hard for her, even for a younger woman, to get my number... to take it and remember it... and she didn't even look like she was trying to write it down or anything, from what I can remember. She was just running around screaming.

NICOLA   What're you trying to say?

STEVE   Eh?

NICOLA   What you saying?

STEVE   What?

NICOLA   Never mind.

STEVE   What's up with you?

NICOLA   Nothing. It doesn't matter.

STEVE   Maybe. I don't know. I could be in the clear. Perhaps they didn't get me number. I could've got away with it, they mightn't have anything on me at all, it all happened so quick.

A loud knocking on the door. STEVE & NICOLA freeze. Steve slowly walks to the door and listens for who's outside. Knock repeated. STEVE backs up quickly. NICOLA looks terrified. They wait. STEVE eventually, cautiously walks back to the door.

STEVE   Who's there?

Pause

STEVE   Hello? Who's out there?

After a moment STEVE slowly opens the door. There is no-one outside. STEVE pops his head out the door, looks left then right. Moves out of sight around the corner. Silence. NICOLA moves to the door.

STEVE   What the... who the fuck... who the fuck are you?

Suddenly STEVE is heard crying out in pain and appears, holding his hand to his face. NICOLA screams as STEVE falls through the door and onto the floor, groaning. PHIL comes in quickly behind him. Blood starts to flow from STEVE'S nose and mouth. PHIL comes up behind STEVE and grabs him by the hair. NICOLA runs into the corner.

PHIL   Come on... you want some... you want some do you... come on then.

STEVE   What the-

PHIL   Don't fuck with me right!

STEVE   I ain't gonna fuck with you. No one's gonna fuck with anyone, no one's gonna do anything.

PHIL punches STEVE hard in the stomach. STEVE collapses in a heap on the floor. PHIL moves around the room in what appears to be a heightened state of euphoria, pumped up with adrenaline.

STEVE Who are you...what...what do you want?

PHIL And to feel that fresh sea breeze across my forehead, under my eyes, in my mouth. And that smell of wild wheat, growing freely. I feel exhilarated, I really feel good, you know, at peace, not mellow, but confident, a kind of euphoria, a contentment.

STEVE Who… what…

PHIL It's at times like this I feel the world is, in fact, a truly wonderful place.

STEVE Look, just take what you want, alright.

PHIL What the fuck do you mean?

STEVE Take anything you want.

PHIL Take anything I want?

STEVE Yea.

PHIL walks quickly up to NICOLA and stands facing her.

PHIL   I hate it when they say that.

NICOLA   What?

PHIL   Take what you want. I'm not a burglar, not a common thief.

STEVE   I...

PHIL   I don't want any of your belongings, your pathetic little possessions. I've got my own. Shit-head.

STEVE   Sorry, I just thought-

PHIL   How do you stick him?

NICOLA   What?

PHIL   Him. How do you stick the prick?

NICOLA   I... don't... I...

PHIL   You don't know do you?

NICOLA   I...

PHIL   Can you not answer the question, is it a bit of a toughie, a difficult question to answer?

NICOLA   I…

STEVE   Look…

PHIL   Shut it. I put it to you, I don't know you, but I put it to you, that you stick this prick because you're scared of him, frightened of what he might do to you if you ever tried to get away from him. Am I right? I'm right aren't I?

                He's a cunt. You know it. You catch yourself looking at him don't you? When he's eating, or watching the telly, or at a party or something, wanting every other woman in the room but you. And you die a little each time. Inside you, a part of you just wants to cry out because deep down you're disgusted by him but you're more disgusted by yourself because you know he doesn't care, doesn't give a shit about you but you hang around anyway because he's made you feel so worthless.

                He's got his little ways, hasn't he?

NICOLA   What?

PHIL   Tell me about his little ways, he must have his little ways, tell me about them.

NICOLA   What... what ways... I... I don't understand... I...

PHIL   Funny little quirks, habits, particular patterns of behaviour, that sort of thing. Ways in which he... expresses himself.

STEVE   Who are you? What do you want?

PHIL   No? No? Really? What about... Does he hit you? A lot a blokes hit women, gives em a hard on, a little stiffy, they get off on the power, the control. Does he do that? Do ya?

PHIL goes to STEVE and yanks him up by the hair

            Well, do ya?

STEVE shakes his head

            He shook his head. Is that true? He's never touched you?

NICOLA slowly nods her head. PHIL smashes STEVE'S head onto the floor.

> Well, well, well. Domestic bliss. How refreshing it is, in these difficult and highly stressful times to come across a couple such as yourselves.
>
> I gatecrashed a party tonight. I like to gatecrash parties because nobody knows who I am, which suits me, because then I can just observe, be on the outside not on the inside. Because once you're on the inside it's very difficult to find your way out. I found myself, for no good reason in a shadowy back bedroom. Suddenly above the distant music I heard voices raised in agitation. I saw a couple enter the bedroom and argue. And a man... slapped and punched the woman in order to... I dunno... get his point across or something... to shut her up anyway. I got the impression that he'd done it before... can't explain it really...just some vibe between them... a sort of understanding... a certain way of communicating they'd developed. She talked. He slapped. She stopped talking. What could be simpler?

To be honest, it quite surprised me, cause I'd spotted the woman earlier on at the party and she seemed to be having a right good time. But she wasn't having a right good time any more. Oh no. To be honest it sort of made me upset, Sort of ruined my evening, so I decided to follow this happy couple when they left the party. He drove off sharpish, and I stayed close enough to watch them from behind. They began to argue again. I could see their silhouettes, their little heads moving up and down agitatedly as they drove along. At one point I got stuck at the lights, an I thought I'd lost them. But as luck would have it I caught up with them again a bit further on down the road and I discovered, to my surprise, that they'd been involved in some kind of accident or commotion. They'd been hit. Or hit someone. All hell was breaking lose. There was an old woman running around screaming and as far as I could see... someone else trapped underneath the car. But what was unusual and rather heartless I thought was that, instead of getting out of the car to see what was going on, the driver, our friend from the party, decides to just piss off, leaving the poor bastard

>   under the car, lying, fucked up in the middle of the road. Very nice.

PHIL grabs STEVE by the hair and yanks him up

>   Well, all I can say is it was a bit a good fortune that I was following behind you, weren't it.

PHIL lays another one on STEVE, who slumps to the floor. PHIL casually walks out the door. NICOLA goes to STEVE and tries to help him. After a moment PHIL re-appears, dragging behind him, a bloody, cut and badly injured man. He dumps the man on the floor. STEVE and NICOLA jump back in horror.

>   I thought about bringing him to the hospital, but then he looked in such bad shape, after his accident an all, I never thought he'd make it. And I thought you might like to see him again, cause you never had much of a chance earlier after driving away so quickly and all.

STEVE   What the fuck... who... who is... for fuck's sake... what...

PHIL   I drove up sharpish after you'd gone, piled him on the back seat, told everyone at the scene it would be quicker if I drove him to

	the hospital in my car. I was gonna take him an all, but then I caught up with you again… an… it sorta… threw me… I wasn't sure what to do for the best.
STEVE	You sick fuck… to do this… to think about doing this…
PHIL	Don't get all holier then thou on me. It's your fault he's like this in the first place.
STEVE	But to… bring him here like this…bring his body here like this… oh God… Oh Christ Almighty.
PHIL	He's your responsibility now.

PHIL walks up to NICOLA

> Take care you. I have to say it though. Your taste in men, it's a bit suspect.

PHIL leaves. STEVE and NICOLA both stare transfixed at the victim on the floor in front of them. They move in for a closer look. Suddenly, the victim groans. They jump back. SLOW FADE.

ACT TWO

Six months later. Late afternoon. NICOLA, is standing, looking out of the window. SID is sitting at a table, drinking a cup of tea.

SID   Any sign?

NICOLA   No, not yet.

SID   Never mind.

Pause

NICOLA   He's never normally this late.

SID   Isn't he?

NICOLA   No.

SID   (*Beat*) Maybe he has gone for that drink after all.

NICOLA   It's possible.

SID   Shame.

NICOLA   Why, will you have to go soon?

SID   (*Checking watch*) Soon-ish.

NICOLA   Yea, if he has gone for a drink, there's no telling what time he might roll in.

SID   Oh.

NICOLA   He has been known to stay out all night.

SID   All night?

NICOLA   Has been known.

SID   (*Beat*) Enjoys a drink then?

NICOLA   Now and again.

SID   Helps him to unwind?

NICOLA   Something like that, yea.

SID   You said he was involved with motor cars in some way, a mechanic?

NICOLA   Did I?

SID   That's what you said.

NICOLA   Yea.

SID   Handy thing to be good with cars I suppose, able to fix them and all that.

NICOLA   Yea, he's always messing about with em.

SID   Is he?

NICOLA   Yea. Always fiddling about under the bonnet. I reckon he thinks more of that car then he does of me.

NICOLA laughs. SID joins in.

SID   Do you drive?

NICOLA   Me?

SID   Yes.

NICOLA   Yea, but he won't let me near it.

SID   Oh?

NICOLA   He says I'm a menace. He says I drive to slow.

SID   Ah. I prefer public transport myself. I think it's safer.

NICOLA   Yea, course.

SID	I mean, I'll get into a car, as long as it's the right person driving. Problem is, alot of people don't have the right attitude.
NICOLA	No.
SID	I speak from experience.

Pause

NICOLA	He'll be sorry he missed ya.
SID	(*Finishes remainder of tea*) Oh, right, yes.
NICOLA	Will you come back another time?
SID	I'd like to. If that's alright?
NICOLA	Yea... I mean... I'm sure he'd like to... meet you... meet up with you.
SID	I hope so.

SID stands. He smiles at NICOLA

NICOLA	I hope you don't think I'm...
SID	What?
NICOLA	Chucking you out or nothing.

SID   That's alright.

NICOLA   I've got to go out myself see.

SID   I understand.

NICOLA   Sorry.

SID   I'm sorry. I didn't mean to take up so much of your time.

NICOLA   As I said, he's more than likely gone for a drink anyway.

SID   Right. Thanks again for the tea.

NICOLA   That's alright.

SID   I just had an impulse to pop over and see you both, that's all.

NICOLA   Sure.

SID   I would have phoned beforehand, if I'd had your number.

NICOLA   Course.

SID   But I was only given the address. I did think of dropping you a line, but I don't think I'd have been able to say, what I wanted to say, in any other way but in person, face to face.

Pause

SID   And well, to be perfectly honest, curiosity did get the better of me. I wanted to see if you were as I'd imagined.

NICOLA   Right.

SID   Just to satisfy my curiosity. Do you mind?

NICOLA   No. No, not at all.

SID   I should imagine there's alot of people who would prefer to remain anonymous in these cases.

NICOLA   Well.

SID   And you're husband? He won't mind?

NICOLA   He'll be fine.

SID   Good.

NICOLA waits for SID to make a move. Instead, he rubs his eyes and drops his head.

NICOLA	You alright?
SID	I'm sorry. It's just that I feel so… I'm sorry.
NICOLA	What… what's the matter… what is it?
SID	I'm so sorry.

SID slumps back down in the chair. NICOLA is unsure how to deal with the situation

SID	Can you… I don't know if you can…
NICOLA	You alright?
SID	I'm sorry really… I'm… can you understand that I'm… I really am in your debt.
NICOLA	No I…
SID	I am really.
NICOLA	Yea, well… that's… nice… you know.
SID	(*Beat*) I feel a bit foolish.
NICOLA	It's OK, honest.

SID   I'm very grateful to you both. I tend to get a bit upset, a little emotional, you know, when I think about it, that night.

NICOLA   Only natural.

SID   Sometimes I can't sleep. I lie awake in bed at night, just staring at the shadows moving across the ceiling, just thinking about it, about what happened, trying to remember, trying to piece together some small fragment, but it's all so confusing, all such a blur.

NICOLA   Is it?

SID   Yes. I've had these flashes, flashbacks. But I can never seem to make sense of anything, everything's jumbled.

NICOLA   Is it?

SID   Yes.

NICOLA   (*Beat*) Maybe you need to just forget, put it all behind you. You're just getting yourself worked up into a state about it.

SID   Yes, you're right. Of course you're right.

	I almost feel I know you. Isn't that weird? Can you understand that?
NICOLA	I don't know I...
SID	I owe you and your husband a great deal.
NICOLA	That's alright.
SID	I was left for dead.
NICOLA	But-
SID	Written off. And you helped me, a complete stranger, brought me to hospital, left me in safe hands, and just took off, vanished into the night, expecting nothing. And now, now that I've found you, hiding away here, because of the sort of people you are, you're trying to play it down, make light of it, as if what you did wasn't important, wasn't, in it's own way, heroic. Thanks to you and your husband I've been given a second chance.

Pause

That's why I've come. To express my gratitude to you both. When you come as close to death as I came, you tend to reevaluate certain things. You and your husband gave me the opportunity to do just that and I wanted to show my appreciation.

The door opens and STEVE enters. He is wearing greasy overalls. He is jangling his car keys.

SID　　　　　Ah.

STEVE　　　Yea?

SID　　　　　Steve?

STEVE　　　(*Regarding SID*) That's right.

SID　　　　　My name's Sidney.

SID walks over to STEVE holding out his hand. STEVE looks quizzically over at NICOLA. SID takes STEVE'S hand in his.

SID　　　　　Hello.

STEVE　　　Hello.

NICOLA　　Do you remember him Steve?

STEVE　　　Remember him from where?

NICOLA   From the accident.

STEVE   Eh?

NICOLA   From the accident, remember?

STEVE   Sorry, you've lost me. What accident?

SID   You helped me.

STEVE   Helped you?

SID   Yes.

STEVE   Don't follow ya.

SID looks across at NICOLA smiling

NICOLA   You remember. That night. Few months ago. In the motor. That bloke we helped. This is the bloke we took to the hospital that night. He'd been run over.

STEVE stares at SID as he realises who's in front of him

SID   I'm sorry, I just turned up tonight. Sorry if I've surprised you. I was going to write to you first but I just suddenly had this overwhelming impulse to see you both.

Pause

	I was just telling your wife how grateful I am for all you've done. I feel like a new man. I've completely recovered.
NICOLA	That's good in it?
SID	I feel wonderful.
NICOLA	He's been here a while.
SID	I've been waiting for you. I thought I'd missed you. Your wife said you'd probably gone for a drink. I was just about to leave, it's lucky I caught you.
STEVE	Yea.
SID	It must be a bit of a shock for you I know, me just turning up here like this, out of the blue, without any warning. I'm sorry if I've surprised you.
NICOLA	He looks better don't he?

STEVE slowly nods his head

SID	I feel fine. I had a nasty bump on my head but that's as good as healed now. (*SID shows the scar to STEVE*) I was in quite a

	bad way at one point, they didn't expect me to pull through at the hospital, but I surprised them.
STEVE	Yea.
SID	The doctor said someone must have been watching over me. My own personal guardian angel looking down on me.

Pause

	I had an urge to just come round and see you and... well, I don't know... see you and say thanks and tell you that I'm grateful for what you did.

Pause

STEVE	You better then?
SID	Yes, thanks to you.
STEVE	Good. Excellent.

Pause

SID	Your wife tells me you're a mechanic.
STEVE	(*Glances at NICOLA*) Yea, that's right.

SID   I saw your car parked out front. It's very nice.

STEVE   It's a good motor.

SID   The black BMW?

STEVE   That's right, yea.

SID   (*Beat*) I don't drive I'm afraid.

STEVE   No?

SID   I stick to public transport. I think it's safer. And my recent experience hasn't done much for my confidence.

STEVE   No, well.

SID   Understandable under the circumstances.

STEVE   Yea.

Pause

SID   Well, as I said. I just had the impulse to come over and see you both. I would have phoned first if I'd had your number, to warn you I'd be coming, but I only had the address.

Pause

STEVE · You say you had the address?

SID · Yes, but no phone number, unfortunately.

STEVE · (*Looking at NICOLA*) I wasn't sure we'd left it.

SID · I had it. As I said to your wife, I would have dropped you a line, but I'm not much of a one for writing down what I want to say, finding the right words and all that.

STEVE · I thought we didn't... I can't remember us leaving... maybe we... did you?

NICOLA · Did I what?

STEVE · Give our details to the hospital?

NICOLA · No.

STEVE · You sure?

NICOLA · Yea.

STEVE · You must have.

NICOLA   No.

STEVE   Yea, you must have.

NICOLA   But I-

STEVE   Dizzy sod. She gets a bit confused.

SID   Well, I'm glad they had it anyway, otherwise I'd never have known who it was who helped me.

          I'm sure there are a lot of people who'd prefer to remain anonymous but I'm glad that's not the case with you. All the same, I'd hate to think I'd barged in on you, you probably want to put that night behind you as much as I do.

STEVE   Well...

SID   I'm sorry. I've probably brought it all back, just turning up like this.

NICOLA   We didn't do that much.

SID   I don't agree. You saved me.

NICOLA   Well em... that's alright... you know.

SID	Who knows what might have happened if you hadn't turned up when you did.

Pause

STEVE	You over the worse then?
SID	Yes, I think so.
NICOLA	Was you in a lot... was you in a lot of pain?
SID	No, not really. I was out cold.
STEVE	So you don't remember much about it?
SID	The accident?
STEVE	Yea.
SID	Last thing I remember seeing was the blinding headlights of the car that hit me, going up in the air and landing on the bonnet. Did you see that?
STEVE	(*STEVE looks at NICOLA*) Na. By the time we got there you'd already been hit.
SID	The police came to the hospital but I couldn't tell them anything and there

	weren't any witnesses, as far as I know. Did they question you?
STEVE	*(*Beat*)* The coppers?
SID	Yes.
STEVE	Where?
SID	At the hospital?
STEVE	(*Beat*) A bit. But we couldn't tell them anything either.
SID	It all happened so quick.
STEVE	Yea.
SID	I'm lucky you came along when you did, otherwise I probably wouldn't have made it.
STEVE	Who knows. If it hadn't been us it would've been someone else more than like.

Pause

STEVE	You got far to get back?

SID   Not too far.

STEVE   Oh.

SID   All the same I'll have to make a move soon. I don't like being out too late anymore. I tend to get a bit nervous these days, which is understandable I suppose.

NICOLA   Right.

SID   It's the traffic. There's so much of it, so much more of it these day's don't you think?

STEVE   There's alot of it alright.

SID   I'd like to try living in the country for a while. My doctor said I should take a complete rest, go away somewhere, have a complete change of environment. I've been getting quite bad headaches lately as a result of the accident.
    I haven't really had a decent night's sleep since. It's these flashes I keep getting. There's no respite. I've tried everything but nothing seems to do the trick. I'm just getting off and suddenly these damn flashes start up again, these flickering images.

STEVE   Images?

SID   Yes.

STEVE   Images of what?

SID   Not sure. It could have something to do with a combination of things. The drugs I've been taking along with the post accident stress I've been suffering. I've never experienced anything like it before. They seem to be connected, these images, with the accident in some way. Particularly afterwards, after I'd been hit. I seem, in these flashes, to go on a sort of journey. I'm travelling somewhere, but I'm not really conscious, I've no idea where I am, I can't really make anything out, but it's as if I'm going on a kind of trip. The funny thing is it's as if I'm not there, not important anyway, not a priority. There are voices, raised voices, an argument of some kind and... and... that's it. My doctor said it wasn't unusual to experience these kind of post accident traumas. He said it was probably connected to the external violence I'd suffered. That would explain it I suppose. It could be something to do with being in hospital, in that environment, around all

                        that sickness, it more than likely
                        encourages those kind of feelings.

STEVE   More then likely.

SID   Yes.

Pause

                        Anyway, I'll be off.

SID walks to the door

STEVE   OK. Go easy, eh.

SID   I'll try. Oh, I almost forgot.

STEVE   What?

SID stops. He smiles at them

SID   I'd like… if I may… to give you
                something. I was hoping I might, because
                of what you did. Just to say thanks. It's
                not much but…

SID Produces an envelope and offers it to STEVE

STEVE   What?

SID	Just a small token.
STEVE	Na, na, na, don't be silly.
SID	Please, it would make me happy.
STEVE	Don't worry about it, honest.
SID	I'd like you to have it.
NICOLA	We don't want nothing.
SID	I want to.
NICOLA	You're better, that's enough.
STEVE	That's right, yea.
SID	But you deserve it.
STEVE	It's nice of ya, but
SID	Please.
STEVE	Eh?
SID	For me.
STEVE	I don't…

SID   You've earned it.

Pause

STEVE   What... what is it?

SID   Take it. From me.

STEVE takes the envelope

NICOLA   Steve.

STEVE   What?

NICOLA   What you doing?

STEVE   What?

NICOLA   You can't take that.

STEVE   He wants us to have it.

NICOLA   But-

STEVE   Don't ya?

SID   Of course.

STEVE   See.

NICOLA   Yea but...

STEVE   What?

NICOLA   We don't...

STEVE   Yea?

NICOLA   We didn't.

STEVE   Yea?

SID   Open it.

NICOLA moves away and sits down. STEVE tears open envelope

STEVE   Well, I didn't... I never did much... I mean... I didn't do nothing nobody else wouldn't have done, know what I mean. I didn't do anything... I mean I didn't... We didn't... do anything for any reward like... This is nice.

He takes out the contents

                It's a cheque. What. You sure about this? It's a cheque... it's a cheque for five thousand quid.

SID   It's yours.

STEVE   I can't take that.

SID   I want you to have it.

STEVE   I can't take it.

SID   I can afford it.

STEVE   You can?

SID   Of course.

STEVE   (*Beat*) Na, you're alright.

NICOLA   Please, we don't want nothing.

SID   If you hadn't come along when you did.

STEVE   Yea but...

SID   Who knows what might have happened.

NICOLA   We didn't...

SID   If I'd had to have waited for an ambulance the doctor I'd probably never have made it.

STEVE   Yea but five grand... I mean... That's a lot of money... I mean you're sure... you're sure you can afford it?

SID   Of course.

STEVE   (*Beat*) If you're sure.

SID   Have a holiday or something.

STEVE   Could do.

SID   Get away from it all for a while.

STEVE   Could do, yea.

SID   Take a break.

STEVE   Could do with it.

SID   Who couldn't.

STEVE   Christ. Five thousand quid. I don't believe it.

Pause

           Hang on a sec.

SID   Yes?

STEVE	You em… you haven't signed it.
SID	Oh. (*Laughs*) Sorry about that.
STEVE	That's OK.

SID takes the cheque signs it and gives it back to STEVE.

SID	There you go.
STEVE	Thank you.
SID	No. Thank you.

Pause

>Well, I really will have to make tracks.

SID walks to the door.   STEVE walks with him.

>Thanks for seeing me and for being so understanding. I know it can't have been easy for you.

| STEVE | That's OK.   You sure about this? |
| SID | Of course. |

STEVE opens the door

	I was thinking. Maybe we could… the three of us… perhaps we could…
STEVE	What?
SID	The three of us… perhaps we could… Well, we'll see. It was nice to meet you.
STEVE	Yea. Likewise. Keep your pecker up, eh.
SID	I'll try.

SID turns to leave. Stops. Turns back.

SID	Oh yes. I almost forgot.
STEVE	What?
SID	How stupid of me.
STEVE	(*Laughs*) What it is now?
SID	I meant to tell you. I meant to tell you before. I had a visitor.

Pause

When I was in hospital.

Pause

                    Nice chap. Said he knew you.

STEVE   Knew us?

SID   He was the one who gave me your address, now I think of it. I'd no idea who he was but he knew you, by the sound of it.

STEVE   Knew us?

SID   By the sound of it.

STEVE   (*Beat*) Don't know.

SID   He seemed to know you.

STEVE   Yea?

SID   Yes.

STEVE   (*Beat*) Can't think.

SID   He knew I'd been in an accident.

STEVE   Did he?

SID   He said he was a friend of yours. He wasn't any friend of mine. Do you remember him?

STEVE looks at NICOLA

        I'd no idea who he was. I'd never seen him before. I thought he might be one of those, special visitors, the hospital sometimes lay on. I didn't tend to get any visitors, you see. He gave me your address, and he said to look out for your black BMW, which is always parked out the front. I saw it on my way in, it's a beautiful car. That was my own little ambulance wasn't it?

STEVE   (*Laughs*) Yea. Yea, I suppose it was.

SID   I remember now. Now I remember. Sorry, how stupid of me. Your friend, the man who came to see me in hospital. He told me, he said, he'd only met you that night, that's it, that's why you can't remember him. He said he'd only met you for the first time at a party earlier that night. The night of the accident.

Pause

        Now, let me think. That's it. He was following behind, behind you, he said he was following behind you in his car, that's how he knew about the accident, of course. Do you remember him now?

Pause

STEVE   At a party?

SID   I think that's what he said. I could be wrong. But I'm pretty sure I'm right.

STEVE looks at NICOLA

STEVE   Do you remember him?

NICOLA Em…

SID   He remembers you.

Pause

STEVE   Yea, yea, I remember, I remember him now. We met that night, course we did. At the party, yea.

STEVE crosses to NICOLA

        You know that bloke.

NICOLA Eh?

STEVE   That bloke. At the party. Remember. You danced with him.

NICOLA	Danced with him?
STEVE	For quite a while.
NICOLA	Did I?
STEVE	Remember?
NICOLA	(*Beat*) Oh yea.
STEVE	Yea, that's right. We invited him back for a nightcap. He was following behind. What my thinking about.
SID	You probably blanked him out.
STEVE	Yea.
SID	What with the accident and all the commotion and everything.
STEVE	That's what I did.
SID	Not surprising really.
STEVE	No.
SID	From what he was saying, if you hadn't come along when you did.

STEVE   Yea, well.

SID   Who knows what might have happened.

STEVE   Yea, well… you just… well you just… react, don't you.

SID   I'm glad you did.

STEVE   Yea. Gotta act quickly. No time to mess about.

SID   Absolutely. Your friend said he was impressed by your professionalism.

STEVE   As I said.

SID   The way in which you didn't panic. Took control of the situation.

STEVE   Suppose.

SID   The way in which you kept your head in a tight spot.

STEVE   Well.

SID   Not scared of a bit of blood and guts. Not afraid to get involved, get stuck in, get your hands dirty, that kind of thing.

STEVE   Yea, well.

SID approaches STEVE

SID   Thought so. You're like me. Injury and death don't bother me. I never turn away at the sight of blood. I mean, we stare death in the face every day, don't we?

STEVE   Do we?

SID   Don't we?

STEVE   (*Beat*) Yea, yea I suppose-

SID   I feel so… I want to run… you know… just… just run, just gallop through oceans of wheat… to feel that… to feel that fresh sea breeze across my forehead… under my eyes… in my mouth. I feel exhilarated… I feel good, you know… at peace… a kind of euphoria… a contentment… at times like this I feel the world is, in fact, a truly wonderful place.

Pause

   I'm actually not afraid to die.

STEVE   No?

SID   No. I mean, I'm thankful, thankful to be alive, don't get me wrong. But I've no fear of death. Why waste time worrying about the inevitable, when it comes, I'll be waiting. I hope that doesn't sound too morbid, I've just got a healthy curiosity, that's all. I often wonder if there's anything else, anything else after this, you know, if there's anything else, or if this is all there is. After we've gone I mean. What do you think?

STEVE   Don't know.

SID   Don't know?

STEVE   Try not to think about it too much.

SID   (*To NICOLA*) But I mean I'd hate to think that this is all there is, wouldn't you? I'd hate to think that you only get one chance, one go at it, wouldn't you? I mean if this is it, well, that just doesn't seem very fair to me, does it you? Well, does it? Nicola?

NICOLA   What?

SID   Does it seem very fair to you that this is all there is?

NICOLA pauses

STEVE   Well, you gotta make the best of it, ain't ya.

SID   I would have found out to, wouldn't I, if you hadn't come along that night. I'd be there now, wouldn't I? Experiencing it for myself.

Pause

STEVE   Look-

SID   Yes?

STEVE   Em-

SID   Yes?

STEVE   We gotta go out.

SID   What?

STEVE   We gotta go out.

SID   Oh.

STEVE   We got to meet someone see.

SID   Sorry, I was rambling.

NICOLA   You could stay. If we didn't have to go out. You could stay as long as you wanted.

SID   That would have been nice.

STEVE   Yea, yea, you could, that's right. It's just that…

SID   You've made other plans?

STEVE   Yea.

SID   Shame.

STEVE   Yea.

SID   We could have gone for a drink, the three of us. Or, if we preferred, we could have got a few bottles in and made a night of it in here. We could become friends, good friends. Maybe, in time, you'd visit me. We could make it a regular fixture, what do you think?

STEVE looks at NICOLA

NICOLA   That would be nice.

SID	We could, if you wanted, become firm friends. We could exchange Christmas and birthday cards, or, if we felt so inclined, give each other little presents now and then, nothing too fancy, just little spontaneous tokens of affection. What do you say?

Pause

STEVE	Yea. Why not.
SID	Really?
STEVE	Yea, whatever.
SID	You don't sound too sure.
STEVE	Well…
SID	You're not just saying it to make me feel better are you?
STEVE	…No, no…
SID	Because people do that to me all the time.
STEVE	What?
SID	Go along with me. Patronise me.

NICOLA   No, not at-

SID   Just to see the back of me.

NICOLA   Look-

SID   Just to get rid of me.

NICOLA   No.

SID   Because I'm not liked.

STEVE   Eh?

SID   Me. People, people don't seem to take to me. I can't explain it. It's just something about me. Vibrations or signals I give off or... I don't understand it... I don't know what I'm doing wrong.

SID walks over to NICOLA

            Do you like me?

NICOLA   Eh?

SID   Do you want me to go?

NICOLA   (*Beat*) No, I...

SID   Or are you just like all the rest?

NICOLA   Excuse me?

SID   Are you? Are you just like all the rest?

STEVE   Going to have to ask you to go now I'm afraid mate.

SID   Do you like me?

NICOLA   Yea.

SID   Do you mean it?

STEVE   I said-

SID   Are you happy?

NICOLA   What?

SID   Happy?

NICOLA   (*Beat*) Suppose so.

STEVE   What is this?

SID   Honestly?

STEVE	What's all this about? What's brought all this on?
SID	Does he make you laugh?
STEVE	Did you hear me?
SID	Or does he make you cry?
STEVE	Hold on a minute.
SID	Are you happy, Nicola?
STEVE	What is all this?
SID	Are you?
STEVE	Excuse me.
SID	I think you might be like... might be like all the rest. I think you might be like him.
STEVE	What was that you said?
SID	You.
STEVE	What about me?
SID	You see-

STEVE   What do you mean? What do you mean by saying that?

STEVE grabs SID'S arm

               What about me? Did you hear me, Oi!

SID turns his back on STEVE

SID   (*TO NICOLA*) Do you understand what I'm saying to you?

STEVE   I don't believe this.

SID   What?

STEVE   You got some front, ain't ya.

SID   Sorry, what?

STEVE   Who the fuck do you think you are anyway?

SID   I'm the victim.

STEVE   What?

SID   Of the accident.

STEVE   Yea.

SID	You helped me.
STEVE	Yea... well... yea... But...
SID	But what?
STEVE	Just remember that alright.
SID	(*Smiling*) How can I ever forget?

Pause. STEVE and SID regard each other

STEVE	Thanks for popping by.
SID	Not a problem.
STEVE	But we've got to-
SID	Yes, you've got to go out.
STEVE	That's right.
SID	So I've got to get out?
STEVE	That's right. Come on, now.
SID	You've got to go out?
STEVE	Wrong! You've got to go out. Out of here. Come on, on your bike.

SID	I haven't got a bike.
STEVE	Piss off!
SID	Maybe you could give me a lift. Like you did that night.

STEVE takes SID'S arm and leads him to the door

	Let go.
STEVE	That's the thanks you get.
SID	Let me go.
STEVE	For helping someone out.
SID	Take your-
STEVE	Doing someone a favour.
NICOLA	Mind out Steve.
STEVE	Come on.
NICOLA	You'll hurt him.
STEVE	Come-
NICOLA	Stop it.

STEVE   Shut it!

NICOLA   Please.

STEVE   I told you girl.

NICOLA   But-

STEVE   I told you.

NICOLA   But-

STEVE   I mean it.

STEVE has SID round the throat

           Now you listen to me you little cunt. I don't know what you want, I don't know what your game is, but I don't want to see your ugly little face around here again, do you understand? Do you?

SID NODS

           We don't wanna see you again. We don't wanna be your friend. We don't want nothing to do with you anymore, right? Right?

SID   Wrong.

STEVE   What?

SID produces a massive gun and points it at STEVE

            What... what the-

SID   Get back.

STEVE   What the fuck-

SID   Down on your knees.

STEVE   What you doing?

SID   Did you hear me?

NICOLA   Please.

STEVE   What's going on... what you-

SID   Shut up.

STEVE   Alright... alright... don't hurt...

SID   On your knees. I won't tell you again.

SID kicks STEVE to the floor

STEVE   Yea, yea... alright, alright. What you gonna do? What you doing? Please...

	shit… don't hurt… please don't hurt me… I didn't mean-

SID   Stop fucking dribbling.

STEVE   Don't.

SID   Be quiet.

STEVE   Please.

SID   I mean it.

NICOLA   Please no.

SID clicks gun off safety hatch

STEVE   No Jesus… oh mother… oh fuck…

SID   Prepare yourself.

STEVE   No.

NICOLA   No, please.

SID   Prepare to meet your maker.

STEVE   NO!

NICOLA   Don't!

SID   Bye, bye.

STEVE   DON'T... NO... for Jesus Christ's sake... don't... don't do this... please... please... I helped you.

SID   Go on.

STEVE   Helped you.

SID   I'm listening.

STEVE   The... the accident... the hospital.

SID   What about it?

STEVE   I...

SID   Yes?

STEVE   I took you.

SID   That's right.

STEVE   I took you. That night.

SID   Yes, you gave me a lift

STEVE   Yes... I...

SID   (*Pushing barrel against STEVE'S head*) You?

NICOLA   Don't!

SID   Go on.

NICOLA   Please.

SID   What did you do?

STEVE   I…

SID   Don't stop.

STEVE   I…

SID   You?

STEVE   I…

SID   Yes?

STEVE   I SAVED YOU!

STEVE collapses onto the floor. SID moves away. NICOLA comforts STEVE.

NICOLA   What do you want?

SID   I wanted to give him a chance.

SID pulls STEVE up by his hair and pushes the barrel of the gun against his head. NICOLA scrambles back, screaming.

                        I want you to tell me what happened. I need you to tell me what happened.

STEVE   It-

SID   Yes?

STEVE   It-

SID   Go on.

NICOLA   It was us. We hit you, we hit you! It was us alright.

SID   You?

NICOLA   Yea. It was our car. We ran you over.

SID   But I thought it was a hit and run?

NICOLA   It was.

SID   But… but you took me to hospital.

NICOLA   We had to.

SID   Had to?

NICOLA   That bloke made us. The one that visited you in hospital. He brought you here. You were half dead. We'd no choice.

SID   So you tried to kill me? Did you try and kill me, shit-head?

STEVE   No.

SID   What?

STEVE   No, I mean.

SID   You're not telling me what I want to hear.

STEVE   But…

SID   Did you try and kill me?

STEVE   No.

SID   No?

STEVE   No, I wasn't driving.

SID   You what?

STEVE That night... I wasn't driving. I'd had too many... I was over the limit... she drove... she said she'd drive... she hit you... she didn't mean it but-

SID She drove.

STEVE Yea.

SID She was driving?

STEVE Yea. Ain't that right? Nicola.

SID walks towards NICOLA

SID She's not saying anything.

STEVE Nicola. Nicky. Tell him. Tell him how it was.

NICOLA I...

STEVE You tell him how it was girl.

SID Tell me how it was Nicky. Tell me how it is Nicky.

Pause

NICOLA I...

SID   Well, Nicola? What's it gonna be?

SID turns and points the gun at STEVE. SID takes out another gun and slides it along the floor to NICOLA

                 Pick it up.   Pick it up, I said.

STEVE   What you doing? What's going on?

SID   Do it.

NICOLA   No.

SID   Then I'll finish it right now. Pick it up.

NICOLA   I can't.

SID   I won't ask you again.

SID digs gun into STEVE'S head

NICOLA   Alright, alright, alright.

NICOLA picks up the gun

SID   That's a good girl.   Not so hard is it?

STEVE   What the fuck you doing? What the fuck's going on?

SID   Shut the fuck up. Come over here and point it.

NICOLA just stares

Come over here and point it, I said.

NICOLA shakes her head

You come over here and point that gun now.

NICOLA, fit to burst, in tears, slowly walks across and points the gun at STEVE

At me.

NICOLA stares in disbelief at SID

At my head.

At my head.

NICOLA   I…

SID   At my head.

NICOLA   I can't.

SID   You better do as I say. I'm giving you the chance to finish what you started.

NICOLA   I can't.

SID   Then I'll shoot this piece of shit right now.

STEVE   Christ.

SID   Shoot me.

NICOLA   But I…

SID   I mean it.

NICOLA   But I…

SID   I mean it.

STEVE   Do it.

SID   I'll count to five. Then I'll shoot the bastard. Your choice. Him or me?

NICOLA, hesitates, unsure what to do

               At my head.

NICOLA   I can't!

SID   I'll count to five. If you haven't done it by then, I'll blow his fuckin brains out. Your choice. One.

STEVE   Do it!

SID   Two.

STEVE   Nicola.

SID   Three.

STEVE   Pull the trigger. Pull the trigger, you bitch!

SID   Four.

STEVE   SHOOT HIM... SHOOT HIM... SHOOT HIM!

SID pulls the trigger but his gun isn't loaded. STEVE slumps to the floor. SID looks across at NICOLA who is still pointing the gun at him, frozen rigid. SID walks to the door, which seems to open of it's own accord, flooding the room with light. He exits. NICOLA begins to turn her gun towards STEVE. They stare at each other. It seems she is about to shoot him. She lowers the gun, turns and walks towards the open door as lights fade.

END